GW00374474

TIGER WORDS
QUOTES & SAYINGS

DAVE RICHARDSON

"I was born in 1950, the year of the (metal) tiger. My mother told me that as a child I had a recurring dream that a large ferocious tiger would leap from the top of the wardrobe and devour me. I don't remember that, but I am obsessed with tigers! Go figure!"

DAVE RICHARDSON

The word "TIGER" comes
from the Persian word "TIGRI
meaning "ARROW"

TIGER
A very large solitary cat with
a yellow-brown coat striped wit
black, native to the forests of As
but becoming increasingly rare

———

Used to refer to someone fierce
determined, or ambitious.

★ TIGER WORDS

Number 27

"One day as a tiger is worth a thousand as a sheep"

Chinese Proverb

"Human beings didn't evolve brains to lie around on lakes. Killing's the first thing we learned. A good thing that we did, or we'd be dead and the tigers would own the earth"

ORSON SCOTT CARD

Number 6

"Now I know why tigers eat their young"

AL CAPONE

"A tiger is a tiger; he has his dignity to preserve even though he isn't aware of it"
RUSKIN BOND

"I have both English bulldog determination and Bengal tiger strength"
BIKRAM CHOUDURY

"The violinist is that peculiarly human phenomenon distilled to a rare potency – half tiger, half poet"
YEHUDI MENUHIN

"The most magnificent creature in the entire world, the tiger is"
JACK HANNA

"I may be a tiger in a cage, but at least I'm not a person trapped in life's prison"
ANTHONY T. HINCKS

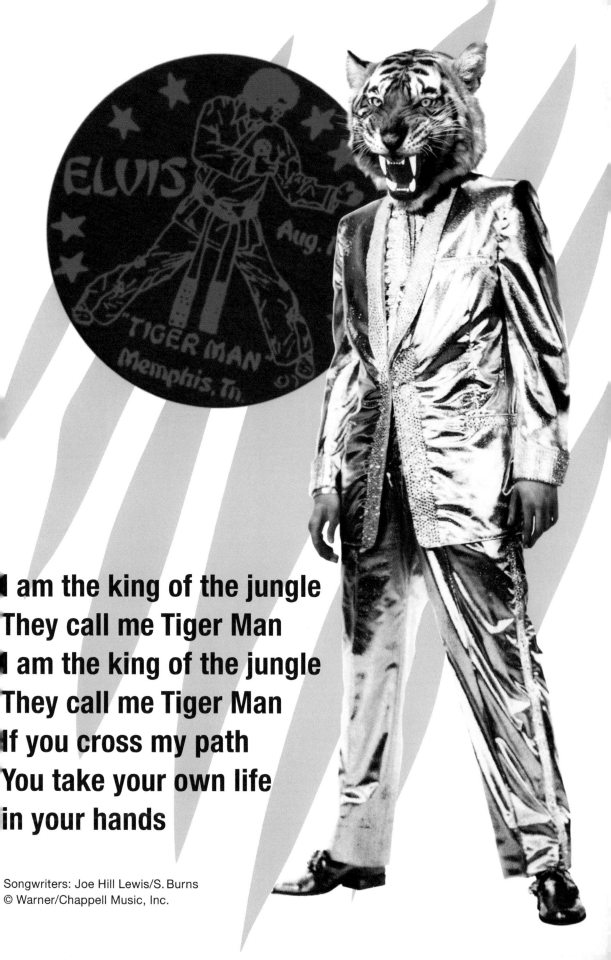

I am the king of the jungle
They call me Tiger Man
I am the king of the jungle
They call me Tiger Man
If you cross my path
You take your own life
in your hands

Songwriters: Joe Hill Lewis/S. Burns
© Warner/Chappell Music, Inc.

"Some people regard private enterprise as a predatory tiger to be shot. Others look on it as a cow they can milk. Not enough people see it as a healthy horse, pulling a sturdy wagon"

WINSTON CHURCHILL

"Dictators ride to and fro upon tigers which they dare not dismount. And the tigers are getting hungry"

WINSTON CHURCHILL

Number 5

"It is no good trying to satisfy a tiger by feeding him cat food"

Winston Churchill

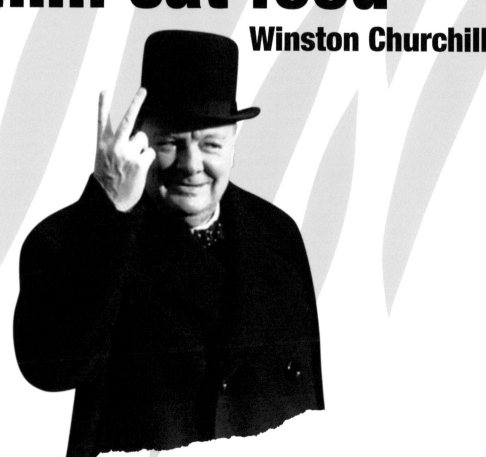

BUCKING THE TIGER

The Faro game was also called "Bucking the Tiger" or "Twisting the Tiger's Tail", a reference to early card backs that featured a drawing of a Bengal tiger. By the mid 19th century, the tiger was so commonly associated with the game that gambling districts where Faro was popular became known as "Tiger Town", or in the case of smaller venues, "Tiger Alley". Some gambling houses would simply hang a picture of a tiger in their windows to advertise that a game could be played there.

PAPER TIGER

A paper tiger refers to a person or thing that appears threatening but is ineffectual.

'The tiger is the royal lord of all animal creation... to me he is the most magnificent expression of animal life"

MABEL STARK

AL.G. BARNES WILD ANIMAL CIRCUS

Miss MABEL STARK AND HER FEROCIOUS GIANT JUNGLE TIGERS

Number 3

"The tiger is more beautiful than the sun"

Muria Proverb

What do tigers dream of?
When they take a
little tiger snooze,
Do they dream
of mauling zebras,
Or Halle Berry in
her Catwoman suit...
Don't worry

ED HELMS – STU'S SONG

© Universal Music Publishing Ltd

"The atom bomb is a paper tiger which the United States reactionaries use to scare people. It looks terrible, but in fact it isn't"

MAO TSE TUNG

"All reactionaries are paper tigers"

Mao Tse Tung

"If you don't enter the tiger's den, how can you catch the tiger's cubs"
BAN CHAO

"A coffee in the morning will turn the most timid of man into a tiger for the rest of the day"
ANTHONY T. HINCKS

"Many people together won't fear a tiger"
CHINESE PROVERB

"When it came to the stylish and graceful art of ballroom dancing, my dad was king of the clubs, a prowling tiger and a wonderfully natural mover"
BRUNO TONIOLI

"Roaring like a tiger turns some children into pianists who debut at Carnegie Hall but only crushes others"
AYELET WALDMAN

WILD THING, YOU MAKE MY HEART SING, YOU MAKE EVERYTHING GROOVY, WILD THING

Songwriter: Chip Taylor
© Sony/ATV Music Publishing LLC

"The time and my intents are more savage, wild; more fierce and more inexorable far, than empty tigers, or the roaring sea"

WILLIAM SHAKESPEARE, Romeo And Juliet

"Once more unto the breach, dear friends, once more, or close the wall up with our English dead! In peace there's nothing so becomes a man as modest stillness and humility; but when the blast of war blows in our ears, then imitate the action of the tiger: stiffen the sinews, summon up the blood"

WILLIAM SHAKESPEARE, Henry V

'O tiger's heart wrapped in a woman's hide"

William Shakespeare

A TIGER CANNOT CHANGE HIS STRIPES

A variation on the more common 'a leopard cannot change his spots', this idiom means people can't change their basic nature.

THE LADY OR THE TIGER

This phrase has its origins in a short story by American writer Frank R. Stockton, 'The Lady, or the Tiger?', first published in 1882. The premise of the story involves an impossible decision (between, you probably guessed, a lady and a tiger), and the phrase has come by extension to refer to a problem that is not solvable.

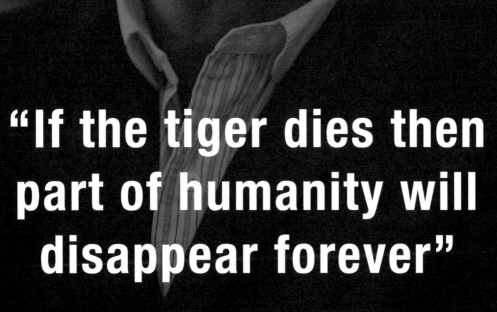

"If the tiger dies then part of humanity will disappear forever"

JEAN-JACQUES ANNAUD

TIGER WORDS

Number 7

"Do not blame God for having created the tiger but thank Him for not having given it wings"

Ethiopian Proverb

NEON TIGER – THE KILLERS

Run neon tiger there's a price on your head

They'll put you down and cut you,

I'll never let them touch you

Away, away, away

Oh I'm gonna need a neon tiger roar

Under the heat of

Under the heat of

Under the heat of

the southwest sun

Neon tiger

There's a lot on

your mind

Songwriters: Brandon Flowers / Dave Brent Keuning /
Mark August Stoermer / Ronnie Jr. Vannucci
© Universal Music Publishing Group

RIDE THE TIGER – JEFFERSON STARSHIP

I want to ride the tiger
I want to sail through the risin' sun for you and you
We got something to learn from the other side
Something to give, we got nothing to hide
I want to ride the tiger.

Look to the summer of seventy-five
All the world is gonna come alive
Do you want to ride the tiger?

Songwriters: Byong Yu, Grace Slick, Paul Kantner
Lyrics © Wixen Music Publishing

TIGER WORDS

Number 31

"He who rides the tiger is afraid to dismount"

Chinese Proverb

"My dad's a Pentecostal Minister, meaning that he's full of charisma. If he's telling a story about Noah's Ark, you best know each tiger is going to be having their own little conversation and narrative"
JOHN BOYEGA

"There is nothing like the thrill of walking through the jungle looking for a tiger and knowing they could be watching you already"
ASHLAN GORSE COUSTEAU

"I have a different constitution, I have a different brain, I have a different heart, I got tiger blood, man"
CHARLIE SHEEN

"Tigers and women! Tigers and women have something in common, it is their disposition; they must be treated majestically!"
HENRIETTA NEWTON MARTIN

"Only those who have been slaves know that in the incense smoke there are tigers"
DANIEL WAMBA

★TIGER WORDS

Number 29

"Time is a river that sweeps me along, but I am the river; It is a tiger that destroys me, but I am the tiger"

JORGE LUIS BORGES

TEACH ME TIGER – MARILYN MONROE

Teach me tiger and I will teeease you
wa wa wa wah
Tiger tiger I want to squeeze you
wa wa wa wah
All of my love I will give to you
But teach me TIGER.. or I'll teach you
Ooh.. tiger .. tiigeeR.. tigrrrR..

Songwriters: April Stevens / Nino Tempo © BMG Rights Management

"Paint stripes on a pig, it does not become a tiger"

George R.R. Martin

TIGER RAG – THE MILLS BROTHERS

Where's that tiger! Where's that tiger!
Where's that tiger! Where's that tiger!
Hold that tiger! Hold that tiger! Hold that tiger!
Choke him, poke him, kick him and soak him!
Where's that tiger? Where's that tiger?
Where oh where can he be?
Low or highbrow, they all cry now
"Please play that Tiger Rag for me"

Songwriters: Edwin Edwards & Antonio Sbarro
© Sony/ATV Music Publishing LLC, Paul Rodriguez Music Ltd.

IT'S A JUNGLE OUT THERE!

"I saw that words can stalk you... A poem
can be both the jungle and the tiger"
RUTH PATEL

"Being a president is like riding a tiger. A man has to keep riding or be swallowed"

Harry S Truman

"Animal totems, like the tiger, come from the other side to protect us while we are away from home"
SYLVIA BROWNE

"Cock-fighting is the popular Malay sport, but the grand sport is a tiger and a buffalo fight, reserved for rare occasions, however, on account of it's expense"
ISABELLA BIRD

"I feel like a tiger right now. There's nothing impossible if you get up and work for it"
MICHAEL FLATLEY

"I definitely have the eye of the tiger. I've fought my way to where I am and will continue to do so"
NICOLE SCHERZINGER

"I was a little tiger, I loved skating. You couldn't get me out of my skates"
TONYA HARDING

TIGER WORDS

Number 13

"There is no off switch on a tiger"

German Proverb

TAME MY TIGER – T.REX

Sister sister
Won't you tame my tiger
Sister sister
Won't you tame my tiger
Won't you give me your love
Real wild

Songwriters: Gloria Richetta Jones / Marc Bolan
© Universal Music Publishing Group, Spirit Music Group

"The human race's prospects of survival were considerably better when we were defenceless against tigers than they are today when we have become defenceless against ourselves"

ARNOLD J. TOYNBEE

TIGER WORDS

Number 15

"No man can tame a tiger into a kitten by stroking it"

Franklin D Roosevelt

ROAR – KATY PERRY

I got the eye of the tiger, a fighter
Dancing through the fire
'Cause I am a champion, and you're gonna
hear me roar
Louder, louder than a lion
'Cause I am a champion, and you're gonna
hear me roar!
Oh oh oh oh oh oh oh oh
Oh oh oh oh oh oh oh oh
Oh oh oh oh oh oh oh oh
You're gonna hear me roar!
Now I'm floating like a butterfly
Stinging like a bee I earned my stripes
I went from zero, to my own hero

Songwriters: Lukasz Gottwald/Max Martin/Bonnie Leigh McKee/Katy Perry/Henry Walter
© Kobalt Music Publishing Ltd., Warner/Chappell Music, Inc, BMG Rights Management

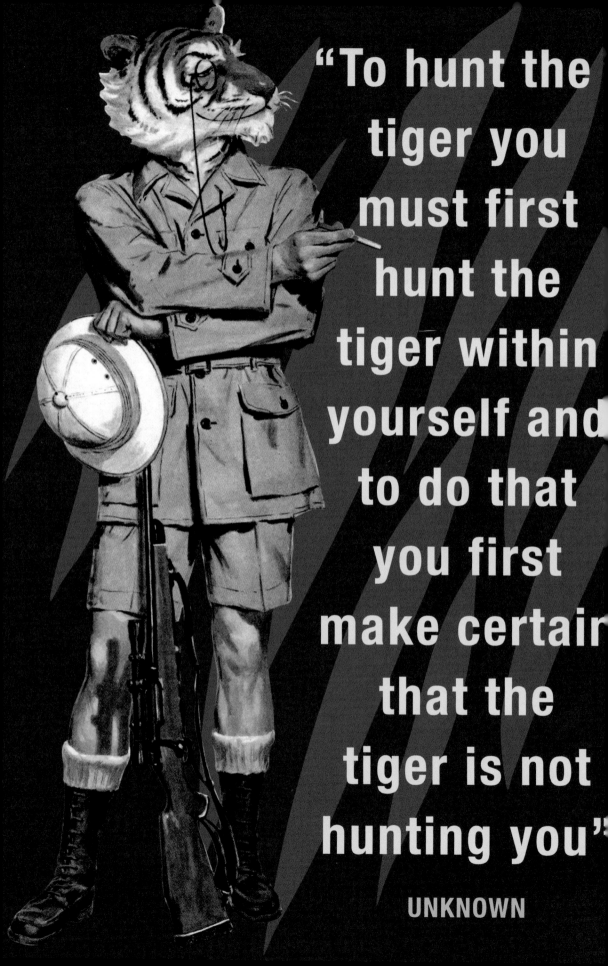

"To hunt the tiger you must first hunt the tiger within yourself and to do that you first make certain that the tiger is not hunting you"

UNKNOWN

"When a man wants to murder a tiger he calls it sport; when a tiger wants to murder him he calls it ferocity"

George Bernard Shaw

"A tiger never returns to his prey
he did not finish off"
CHINESE PROVERB

"Instead of holding a man, the cage held
a tiger, and that tiger's name was Hope.
Williams produced a key that unlocked
the cage and the tiger was out, willy-
nilly, to roam his brain"
STEPHEN KING, Different Seasons

"Our noblest hopes grow teeth and
pursue us like tigers"
JOHN GARDNER

"When I work I am pure as an angel
tiger and clear is my eye and hot
my brain and silent all the whining,
grunting piglets of the appetites"
MARGE PIERCY

"The secret about tigers, he said
blinking owlishly, is that tigers bounce"
ALYSSA DAY, Dead Eye

"Every woman should have
four pets in her life.
A mink in her closet,
a Jaguar in her garage,
a tiger in her bed,
and a jackass who pays
for everything"

PARIS HILTON

TIGER WORDS

Number 17

"The tiger that has tasted blood is never sated with the taste of it"

Spanish Proverb

I'M A TIGER – LULU

A lot of men have come my way
Thinking that I'm easy prey
But you'll never tame this child
She loves running wild
You won't cage me in
Just stick around, let the fun begin
I'm a tiger, I'm a tiger, I'm a tiger, I'm a tiger
I'm a tiger, I'm a tiger, I'm a tiger, I'm a tigerrr

Songwriters: Marty Wilde / Ronnie Scott
© Universal Music Publishing Group, BMG Rights Management

HAVE A TIGER BY THE TAIL

To have a tiger by the tail refers to the act of having 'embarked on a course of action that proves unexpectedly difficult but that cannot easily or safely be abandoned'. Similar to this phrase is the Chinese proverb 'He who rides a tiger is afraid to dismount', which gave rise to the phrase ride the tiger.

PUT A TIGER IN YOUR TANK

Although this phrase may have started life as a 1965 advertising campaign for the Esso Petroleum Company (the company's mascot, now known as Exxon Mobil, is a tiger), the phrase has come to mean 'to invest one with energy or "go"'.

'Van Gogh would have sold more than one painting if he'd put tigers in them"

Bill Watterson

"Behind this door could be a beautiful woman, and behind the same door could be a tiger, you know? You don't know"
JOE CARNAHAN

"The tiger is humbled by memories of prey"
STEVEN ERIKSON

"If you wish to meet and speak with God, you must first try to tame a wild tiger with a feather and a stick"
ANTHONY T. HINCKS

"If you rile a tiger, he's going to show his claws"
ROB JAMES-COLLIER

"Tigers cannot afford to care about what sheep think"
MATSHONA DHLIWAYO

"Would you like to sin with Elinor Glyn on a tiger skin?"

"A madness of tender caressing seized her. She purred as a tiger might have done, while she undulated like a snake" ELINOR GLYN

"The tiger relies on the forest. The forest relies on the tiger"

Cambodian Proverb

"The tigers of wrath are wiser than the horses of instruction"

Tyger! Tyger! burning bright
In the forests of the night
What immortal hand or eye
Could frame thy fearful symmetry?

WILLIAM BLAKE

RIDE THE TIGER – NOEL GALLAGHER

Someday you might find your hero
Some say you might lose your mind
I'm keeping my head down now for the summer
I'm out of my mind but I'm falling in love
I'm going to take that tiger outside for a ride
What a life

Songwriter: Noel Gallagher
Lyrics © Sony/ATV Music Publishing LLC

Number 20

"The tiger springs in the new year. Us he devours"

T S Eliot

There was a young lady of Niger
Who smiled as she rode on a Tiger;
They came back from the ride
With the lady inside
And the smile on the face of the Tiger

WILLIAM COSMO MONKHOUSE

"There never yet has been a country which became powerful without knowledge. A man by his own strength alone cannot successfully combat a tiger, but by his intelligence. he can devise means to entrap him" ZHANG ZHIDONG

Number 9

"Khrushchev reminds me of the tiger hunter who has picked a place on the wall to hang the tiger's skin long before he has caught the tiger. This tiger has other ideas"

John F Kennedy

"I want to be a tiger"
MIGUEL CABRERA

"The rolling of the tiger's eye, while he was devouring the massive lump of meat and bone....seemed to possess the brilliancy as well as the rapidity of lightning"
ALFRED BUNN

"Life is a tiger you have to grab by the tail, and if you don't know the nature of the beast it will eat you up"
STEPHEN KING, Different Seasons

"Apparently, I used to bite, scratch and growl when I was young, so my parents named me Tiger"
TIGER SHROFF

"You can shoot the tiger, or stay out of his way, but you cannot pronounce him a vegetarian"
RICHARD MITCHELL

TIGER WORDS

Number 8

"When the tiger kills, the jackal profits"

Afghan Proverb

JIM CORBETT, MAN-EATERS OF KUMAON

"Tiger is a large-hearted gentleman with boundless courage and that when he is exterminated – as exterminated he will be unless public opinion rallies to his support – India will be the poorer, having lost the finest of her fauna"

"The steel blue of the fern-fringed pool where the water rests a little before cascading over rock and shingle to draw breath again in another pool more beautiful than the one just left – the flash of the gaily coloured kingfisher as he breaks the surface of the water, shedding a shower of diamonds from his wings as he rises with a chirp of delight, silver minnow held firmly in his vermillion bill – the belling of the sambhar and the clear tuneful call of the chital apprising the jungle folk that the tiger, whose pug marks show wet on the sand where a few minutes before he crossed the river, is out to search of his dinner"

"Tigers, except when wounded or man-eaters, are on the whole very good-tempered"

JIM CORBETT

IT'S UP TO US

NO ONE IS COMING

"I am by no means sure that if a man kept a tiger, and lightning broke his chain, and he got loose and did mischief, that the man who kept him would not be liable"

B BRAMWELL

TIGER WORDS

Number 12

"Sit atop a mountain & watch the tigers fight"

Chinese Proverb

"So a pussycat wants to fight a tiger"
MIKE TYSON

"Rocky has only got two halfway decent purse
so far, and it was like a tiger tasting blood"
AL WEILL, MARCIANO'S MANAGER

"I was a tiger, a good fighter, in good shape"
GEORGE FOREMAN

BLIND TIGER

A North American English term for an illegal bar, the term blind tiger first appeared in the mid-19th century, probably because illegal bars, in order to avoid prohibition laws, were disguised as exhibition locales for natural curiosities.

TIGER ECONOMY

A tiger economy (also known as a tiger) refers to a dynamic economy in a small country, especially in East Asia, such as Taiwan, South Korea, and Singapore. The Irish economy was known as the 'Celtic Tiger' during a period of rapid growth in the late 1990s.

EYE OF THE TIGER – SURVIVOR

Risin' up, back on the street
Did my time, took my chances
Went the distance, now I'm back on my feet
Just a man and his will to survive

It's the eye of the tiger, it's the thrill of the fight
Risin' up to the challenge of our rival
And the last known survivor stalks his prey in the nigh
And he's watchin' us all with the eye of the tiger

Songwriters: Frank Sullivan / Jim Peterik
Lyrics © Sony/ATV Music Publishing LLC,
Warner/Chappell Music, Inc

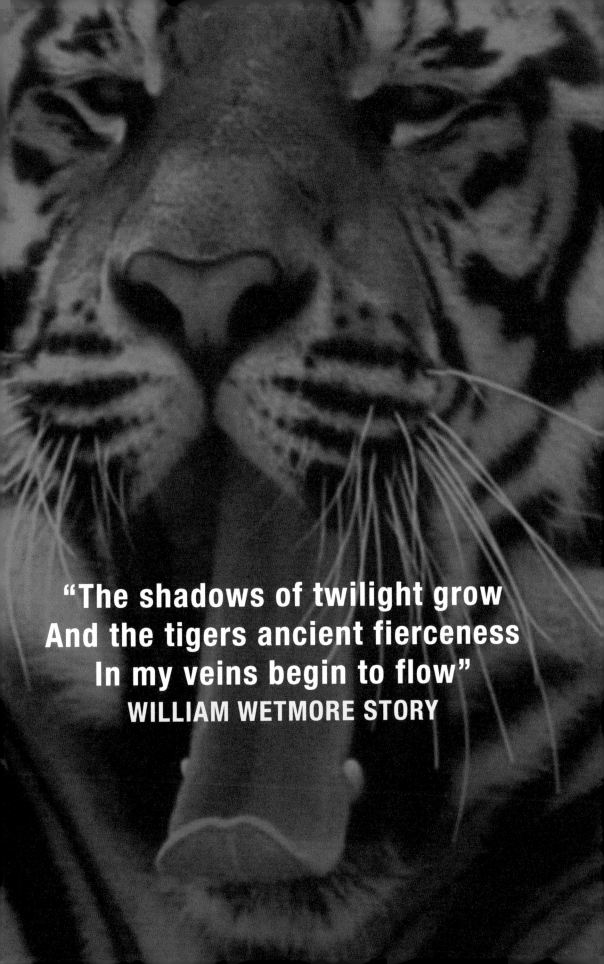

"The shadows of twilight grow
And the tigers ancient fierceness
In my veins begin to flow"
WILLIAM WETMORE STORY

★TIGER WORDS

"Tigers die and leave their skins; people die and leave their names"

Japanese Proverb

"The tigress is a truly majestic creature. She is the alpha animal in the jungle and for good reason. She moves with a fluid grace that no other animal can match. Padding silently, she can creep up on any creature and kill them with a single swipe of her outsized paws. Once those thorn shaped claws rip at you, it is all but over. She is phantom silent and melts into the bush like molten gold into a cast. When she finds a good ambush site, she lurks in the shadows. Then she waits for prey to pass, observing everything with her glittering, feline eyes. When her target appears, she pounces with a coiled energy that is both fearsome and pitiless.

That is why many explorers and adventurers speak of having fear in the jungle. It is a vast supermarket of food and man-meat is on the menu also. The saw-toothed leaves of the jungle drip with rain and menace alike"

LIAM O'FLYNN

TIGER – ABBA

The city is a jungle, you better take care
Never walk alone after midnight
If you don't believe it you better beware
Of me

I am behind you, I'll always find you, I am the tiger
People who fear me never go near me, I am the tiger

Songwriters: Benny Andersson, Björn Ulvaeus
Lyrics © Sony/ATV Music Publishing LLC, Universal Music Publishing Group

Number 25

"If the tiger sits, do not think it is out of respect"

Nilotic Proverb

"Don't hide in the trees
when you know tigers can climb"
ANTHONY T. HINCKS

"I'm a tiger made out of
a paper towel, and I'm going
to wipe you out"
JAROD KINTZ

"In nature a dangerous tiger
deserves a good day"
UNKNOWN

"A hero only appears once
the tiger is dead"
BURMESE PROVERB

"If I produce a 450 pound
Bengal tiger, it's going to create
a lot more wonder than if
I produce a rabbit"
DOUG HENNING

TIGER FEET – MUD

Yeah, yeah
All night long, you've been looking at me
Well you know you're the dance hall cutie
that you love to be
Oh well now, you've been laying it down
You've got your hips swinging out of bounds
And I like the way you do what you're doin' to me

Alright
That's right, that's right, that's right,
that's right I really love your tiger light
That's neat, that's neat, that's neat,
that's neat, I really love your tiger feet

Songwriters: Michael Donald Chapman / Nicholas Barry Chinn
Tiger Feet lyrics © Universal Music Publishing Group

Number 22

"An infallible method of conciliating a tiger is to allow oneself to be devoured"

Konrad Adenauer

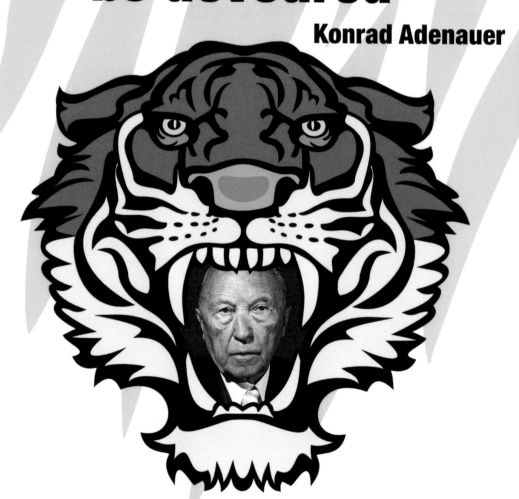

TIGER — FABIAN

TIGER AND
TIGER BOY

I'm your tiger and you're my mate
Hurry up, buttercup, and don't be late
I might get mad if I have to wait
Come right now 'cause I'm on the prowl

Like a tiger, ooh, ooh, ooh, like a tiger
Ooh, ooh, ooh, just to see you smile nearly
drives me wild
I want to growl wow!

Songwriter: Ollie Jones
Lyrics © Sony/ATV Music Publishing LLC, Warner/Chappell Music, Inc.

TIGER MOTHER

A Tiger Mother refers to a 'strict or demanding mother who pushes her children to high levels of achievement', in particular using childrearing methods regarded as typical of China and other areas of East Asia. The term was coined by Amy Chua in her 2011 book Battle Hymn of the Tiger Mother.

TIGER'S MILK

Alcohol-related tiger idiom, Tiger's Milk is a slang term for gin. It's also the name of a Slovenian dessert wine made from overripe grapes.

To feed the ambition in your heart is like carrying a tiger under your arm"

Chinese Proverb

"If a man proves too clearly and convincingly to himself ... that a tiger is an optical illusion – well, he will find out he is wrong. The tiger will himself intervene in the discussion, in a manner which will be in every sense conclusive" LORD BYRON

TIGER WORDS

Number 23

"The impact of an attacking tiger can be compared to that of a piano falling on you from a second story window"

John Vaillant

"Do not seek to escape from the flood by clinging to a tiger's tail"
CHINESE PROVERB

"It is not part of a true culture to tame tigers, any more than it is to make sheep ferocious"
HENRY DAVID THOREAU

"A man's good name is as precious to him as it's skin is to a tiger"
JAPANESE PROVERB

"There has to be absolute trust between the tiger and it's master, but the master must be the master – there must be no mistake about that"
RIDLEY SCOTT

"Wooing the press is an exercise roughly akin to picnicking with a tiger. You might enjoy the meal, but the tiger always eats last"
MAUREEN DOWD

Number 26

"Tigers and deer do not stroll together"

American Proverb

RIDE THE TIGER – BOO RADLEYS

I don't really need to be the way I are
I don't really need to always go so far
I could get by on being alive but having no life
I don't really need a fuel infected car
I don't really need (or want) to be some kind of star
I could get by on being alive but having no life
You don't really know what it is you ask
All that I want is to find some peace at last
Take it further
Ride the tiger

Poem by: Geoff Bird

Number 18

"You know tigers are very unpredictable"

Suraj Sharma

"It is not easy to get rid of an illusion. It lingers eve[n] after the attainment of knowledge. A man dreamed o[f] a tiger, then he woke up and his dream vanished, bu[t] his heart continued to palpitate"
from TALES AND PARABLES OF SRI RAMAKRISHNA

"An oppressive government
is more to be feared than a tiger"
CONFUCIUS

"The child of a tiger is a tiger"
HAITIAN PROVERB

"If you are losing a tug of war
with a tiger, give him the rope
before he gets to your arm.
You can always buy a new rope"
MAX GUNTHER

"Don't strike a flea on a tiger's head"
CHINESE PROVERB

"Never scratch a tiger with
a short stick"
GORDON JACKSON

"In me the tiger sniffs the rose"

SIEGFRIED SASSOON

TIGER COUNTRY

In New Zealand and Australian English, the term Tiger Country refers to 'remote and inaccessible parts of a country', i.e. 'The construction of that road through some very difficult tiger country is now under way'.

EYE OF THE TIGER

One of the best-selling singles of all-time, the hard rock song 'Eye of the Tiger' by the American band Survivor has become a go-to anthem during sporting events. In popular culture, the eye of the tiger has come to symbolize a feeling of power or confidence.

"The first voice they hear is mine, the first touch they feel is mine, the first human face they see is mine. They just think I'm a strange tiger who walks on two legs"

ROY HORN

Number 21

'Every dog is a tiger in it's own street"

Indian Proverb

MY STREET

SEND AWAY THE TIGERS
MANIC STREET PREACHERS

There's no hope in the colonies
So catch yourself a lifeline
Things have gone wrong too many times
So catch yourself a slow boat to China

Fixing some holes from the tigers claws
All your tears will be trembling
Stick those teeth into my back
Seasonal beasts keep them at bay

Can't something go right
Little things change people's lives
Hostile words won't fill your eyes
Same noise left too destroy

Loathsome smile head full of forever's
Will tomorrow bring some perfection
The zoos been overrun in Baghdad
Tiger's claws still in my back

So send away the tigers
Because we're lonely and we're desperate
So send away the tigers
Because they're creeping up and dangerous

Songwriters: James Dean Bradfield/Nicholas Allen Jones/Sean Moore
Lyrics © Sony/ATV Music Publishing LLC

"It is the silence between the notes that makes the music; it is the space between the bars that holds the tiger"

OLD ZEN SAYING

Number 32

"Oh, the tiger will love you. There is no love sincerer than the love of food"

GEORGE BERNARD SHAW

YEAR OF THE TIGER – ST. VINCENT

When I was young
Coach called me the tiger
I always had
A knack with the danger
Living in fear in the year of the tiger

Songwriters: Anne Erin Clark/Sharon Clark
Lyrics © BMG Rights Management

"A tiger does not have to proclaim its tigritude"
NIGERIAN PROVERB

"You handle depression in much the same way you handle a tiger"
DR. R.W. SHEPHERD

"When you starve with a tiger, the tiger starves last"
GRIFFIN'S THOUGHT

"Where there are no tigers, a wildcat is very self-important"
KOREAN PROVERB

"To anger female voters in America is to tread on the tiger's tail"
HENRY ROLLINS

"The bleating of the lamb merely arouses the tiger"
FRENCH PROVERB

Number 33

"Easy tiger"

A SELECTION OF IMAGES FEATURED IN THIS BOO
PLUS LOADS OF OTHER TIGER DESIGNS
ARE AVAILABLE ON T-SHIRTS, POSTERS,
PHONE CASES, CUSHIONS, MUGS, POSTCARDS,
LAPTOP SKINS, etc, etc, AVAILABLE FROM
www.redbubble.com/people/tigerrific

MORE BOOKS FROM THE TIGERRIFIC COLLECTION NOW AVAILABLE FROM AMAZON STORES WORLDWIDE

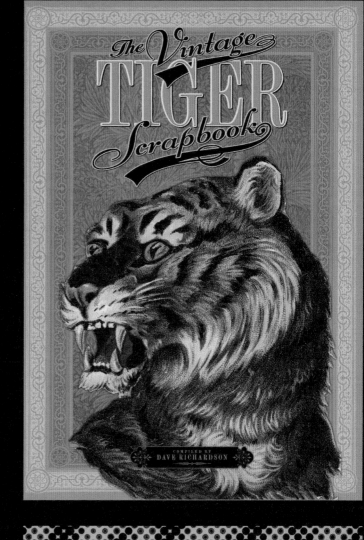

The Vintage TIGER Scrapbook

COMPILED BY DAVE RICHARDSON

WILD STRIPES

DAVE RICHARDSON

ART DIRECTION Dave Richardson DESIGN Julia Kennedy
Copyright © TIGERRIFIC PRODUCTIONS LTD 2018

All images are from the Dave Richardson Tigerrific Collection. The copyright in all original items is retained by the individual publishers, artists, writers, art directors, designers, illustrators and photographers. Every attempt has been made to obtain copyright clearance on all images contained herein. Any omissions please contact the publisher so this can be rectified in future editions.

Congratulations to all the creatives, companies, teams and individuals, throughout time and from every part of the world, who have successfully chosen to use the peerless image of the tiger.

The right of Dave Richardson to be identified as the author of this work has been asserted by him in accordance with the copyright, design and patents act, 1988.

This book is sold subject to the condition that it shall not, by way of trade or otherwise, be lent, resold, hired out or otherwise circulated without the publisher's prior written consent in any form of binding or cover other than that in which it is published.

TIGERRIFIC

"WANTS **YOU**"

TO HELP SAVE ANIMALS IN THE WILD!

GOD SAVE THE TIGER

Reproduced to change WORLD OPINION

34251400R00058

Printed in Poland
by Amazon Fulfillment
Poland Sp. z o.o., Wrocław